Made in the
USA
Middletown, DE

75008595R00057